Our
Constitution

I KNOW AMERICA

Linda Carlson Johnson

947878

THE MILLBROOK PRESS
Brookfield, Connecticut

Published by The Millbrook Press
2 Old New Milford Road
Brookfield, CT 06804
© 1992 Blackbirch Graphics, Inc.

5 4 3 2

Created and produced in association with Blackbirch Graphics.
**Series Editor:** Bruce S. Glassman

**Library of Congress Cataloging-in-Publication Data**
Johnson, Linda Carlson, 1949–
    Our Constitution / Linda Carlson Johnson
    (I know America)
    Includes bibliographical references and index.
    Summary: Describes the creation of the document which sets out the rules
of government for our country.
    ISBN 1-56294-090-2 (lib. bdg.)        ISBN 1-56294-813-X (pbk.)
    1. United States—Constitutional history—Juvenile literature.   2. United
States—Constitutional law—Juvenile literature.   [1. United States—
Constitutional Convention (1787).   2. United States—Constitutional history.
3. United States—Constitution.]   I. Title.   II. Series.
KF4541.Z9J64   1992
342.73'02–dc20                                                         91-43232
                                                                           CIP
                                                                           AC

**Acknowledgments and Photo Credits**
Cover, pp. 23, 26: National Archives; Back cover: ©Tom Doody/The
Picture Cube; pp. 4, 45: ©Stephen R. Brown/National Archives; p. 6:
Library of Congress Collection; pp. 8, 10, 22, 32: The National
Portrait Gallery, Smithsonian Institution; pp. 11, 18, 19, 21, 29, 31,
42: North Wind Picture Archives; p. 12: ©Richard Frear/National
Park Service; p. 17: AP/Wide World Photos; p. 25: The Bettmann
Archive; p. 37: ©Ron Smith/Gamma-Liaison; p. 39: ©Stuart
Rabinowitz; p. 40: ©Markel/Gamma-Liaison; p. 43: AP/Wide World
Photos; p. 44: Architect of the Capitol.

Photo Research by **Inge King**.

# CONTENTS

# We the People

## Article. 1.

# INTRODUCTION

What makes the United States different from most other nations on Earth? You might answer, "We live in a free country." Or you might answer, "People in the United States have more rights than most other people."

But where do those ideas of freedom and the rights of people come from?

They come from a document called the United States Constitution. This document sets out rules for how our government works. And it lists important rights that U.S. citizens have by law.

The Constitution was written more than two hundred years ago by fifty-five men in a room in Philadelphia. The Constitution worked then because it had the support of Americans who believed in its idea of a democracy that protects people's rights. The Constitution will continue to live and grow only as long as we cherish it.

*Opposite:*
The Constitution as it appeared in the final handwritten draft.

5

# C H A P T E R

## 1

# A NEW NATION STRUGGLES TO SURVIVE

Today, the United States is known as one of the most powerful nations in the world. As U.S. citizens, we enjoy more freedom than most people in the world enjoy. Yet the United States, at just over two hundred years old, is a very young nation compared to many other nations in the world.

Before 1776, there was no United States of America. Instead, there were thirteen American colonies ruled by Great Britain. For about 150 years, British kings or queens had ruled these colonies. For most of that time, the American colonists didn't mind British rule. The British, after all, lived far away across the Atlantic Ocean. British governors were supposed to be in charge of the colonies, but these governors usually didn't cause any trouble for the people. The colonies grew in population and wealth under British rule. The American colonists considered themselves British subjects with all the freedoms of people living in Great Britain.

But in the middle of the 1700s, the colonists found out that England didn't think of them as full British citizens. The British government had borrowed a great deal of money to fight a long war with France. The king decided to put taxes on many items shipped to the American colonies. These taxes would raise money for the British government.

The American colonists became angry. They felt cheated because they had not voted for these taxes. The British Parliament was made up of members who were elected by the people of Great Britain, not the people of the American colonies. The colonists complained loudly about this "taxation without representation."

The situation became worse and worse. The British dropped some taxes, but soon put new ones in their place. The colonists became angrier. Many called for war against Great Britain. Soon British soldiers arrived to enforce British rule. The sight of red-

Thomas Jefferson wrote America's Declaration of Independence in 1776. It was our nation's first great document of freedom.

coated British troops marching in their streets made the colonists even angrier. Fighting between colonists and British soldiers broke out in Massachusetts in April of 1775. In 1776, leaders of the thirteen colonies met in Philadelphia. One of the leaders, Thomas Jefferson, wrote the Declaration of Independence, which said the colonies were free of British rule.

But true freedom didn't come without a bloody war, the American Revolution. In 1777, a year after the signing of the Declaration of Independence, the leaders of the colonies signed an agreement called the Articles of Confederation. This document drew the thirteen former colonies together into one nation to fight against a common enemy, the British.

When the war ended in 1781, there was no longer an enemy to fight, and the states wanted to go their own ways. During the war, most of them had formed new governments. The Articles of Confederation set up a central government for all the states, but this government didn't have much power. Under the Articles, each state had one vote in a Congress. The main purpose of this Congress was to control America's relationships with other nations. Congress was also supposed to set up ways to repay the money that the colonies had borrowed from other nations to fight the war against the British.

But the Articles of Confederation didn't give the Congress any power to raise money. Americans had fought a war over taxes that a big government across the ocean had tried to make them pay. They feared

Alexander Hamilton was strongly in favor of writing a constitution for our new nation.

that a big government of the thirteen states could turn out to be just as bad as the British government.

With no power to raise any money, Congress could do little to keep the new nation together. Soon, representatives of the states didn't even show up at meetings of Congress. The thirteen states began to operate as if they were separate nations. Some issued their own money. This money often couldn't be used in neighboring states. Each state made its own laws about how business and trade should be run. Many states also made claims on western lands.

Soon there were fights among the states over many of these issues. Leaders in many colonies began to realize that some kind of new central government was needed. Otherwise, the people of the United States might soon be at war again—this time against one another.

Finally, in September of 1786, two important leaders of the new nation called for a meeting in Philadelphia the next May. These leaders were James Madison of Virginia and Alexander Hamilton of New York. They said the purpose of the meeting was to make changes in the Articles of Confederation. But many experts say that Madison and Hamilton had a grander plan in mind—to form a strong, united nation. Yet even Madison and Hamilton could not know that this meeting would become one of the most important meetings in American history. At this meeting, a group of just fifty-five men would eventually write the United States Constitution.

# SHAYS' REBELLION: A SPARK FOR CHANGE

After the Revolutionary War ended, Americans in many states were against any kind of national government. But a bloody incident in Massachusetts changed many people's minds.

In 1786, some merchants in Massachusetts set out to collect debts owed to them by farmers. The farmers didn't have the money to pay their debts. The angry merchants threatened to take away the farmers' land. If the farmers refused to give up their land, they would go to prison.

The farmers decided to fight for their land. A farmer named Daniel Shays, a former captain in the Revolutionary War, led the rebellion. The armed farmers attacked courthouses and other buildings. They also beat up lawyers, judges, and merchants.

**Shays' Rebellion**

Massachusetts didn't have many soldiers to fight against the farmers' attacks. There was an outcry for the Congress of America to help, but Congress had little money or troops. Finally, a Massachusetts militia put the rebellion down in Springfield. Later, some merchants helped to raise another militia that defeated more forces from the rebellion. Although Shays was beaten, news of the farmers' revolt shocked many Americans. Suddenly they realized that without a strong central government, the people could make their own laws—with guns. The farmers' revolt, which came to be called Shays' Rebellion, convinced many leaders of the states that they needed to think seriously about working together to form a stronger union.

# CHAPTER 2

# A MEETING OF MINDS IN PHILADELPHIA

The big meeting in Philadelphia was planned to begin on May 14, 1787. Two of the *delegates* (people sent by their states) arrived early. One was James Madison, who had called for the convention. The other was George Washington, the most important American general of the Revolution. Washington hadn't wanted to attend the convention at all. He had planned to spend the rest of his life running Mount Vernon, his large farm in Virginia. But a flood of letters arrived at Mount Vernon urging him to come to the meeting.

The rest of the delegates straggled into the city. Some had long distances to travel by horseback or by horse-drawn coach. Some had businesses or farms to take care of. Rain and muddy roads slowed some of

*Opposite:*
The Pennsylvania Statehouse, now called Independence Hall, served as the meeting place for the members of the convention.

13

them down.  There were so many latecomers that the opening session of the convention had to be delayed until May 25.

The men who met in the small Pennsylvania Statehouse for the next four months were an unusual group.  Few Americans in those days were well-educated, yet twenty-nine of the fifty-five delegates to the convention had college degrees.  Many of them were lawyers and doctors, politicians and merchants, farmers and judges.  The youngest delegate was Jonathan Dayton, a twenty-six-year-old lawyer.  The oldest delegate was Benjamin Franklin, at eighty-one.  Franklin, the president of Pennsylvania's executive council, was a famous inventor and statesman.  But Franklin was very ill at the time of the convention.

During the four months the convention lasted, delegates often had to leave to take care of business at home.  On most days, about thirty men were in the convention hall.  The men sat three or four to a table around the room.

## George Washington Sits Up Front

The first action the delegates took was to elect George Washington president of the convention.  Everyone at the meeting— and in the country—respected and loved Washington.  Some people say the creation of the Constitution would never have succeeded if he had not been there. During the convention, Washington seldom spoke.  But everyone felt his presence.

Another important action was taken early in the convention. The delegates agreed that everything that went on in the hall had to be kept secret. They were afraid that they would not be able to speak freely if they knew that their words would later be repeated and criticized by the American people.

Would this rule be taken seriously? George Washington wanted to make sure that it would be. One day, a convention document was found on the ground outside the hall. Someone then gave it to Washington. Before the end of the day's meeting, the general stood up. He said that he was disappointed that someone had been so careless as to drop the paper. He said in a serious voice, "I know not whose paper it is, but there it is. Let him who owns it take it." Then he bowed and walked stiffly from the room.

No one claimed the paper. But the delegates had learned their lesson. In the future, they would keep their discussions secret.

Then the real work of the convention began.

## What Was the Job of the Convention?

What had the delegates to the convention really come to Philadelphia to do? Would they just make a few changes in the Articles of Confederation? Or would they create a completely new form of government?

Many delegates had come to the convention because they were convinced that a new government had to be formed. But what kind of government would it be?  Most of the delegates had very definite ideas.  They had all learned lessons from history about the kinds of governments that didn't work.  And they had at least one example of a government that had worked pretty well.

• The delegates knew of many lands where kings or other rulers, with no laws to guide them, became cruel.  In Turkey, for example, the ruler's power came from his control over the army, and the ruler often used the army to make people obey.

• The delegates also knew of countries in which the people elected lawmakers, but the king could overrule them.  In countries such as France, Spain, and Russia, people were allowed freedom as long as they didn't get in the ruler's way.  But rulers who didn't like what the people decided to do could use their power to stop them.

• The delegates also knew of a few countries in which the power of kings had been controlled by the people.  The best example of this was the British government.  Over many centuries, the British people had gained rights from their British kings and queens.

In 1215, more than five hundred years before the convention in Philadelphia, England was ruled by a king named John.  The nobles in King John's court became angry with him for the way he used his power.  They demanded that King John sign a paper that gave the nobles certain rights.  King John refused.  But he gave in when the nobles threatened to take over the country.

## The Magna Carta

The paper King John signed was called the Magna Carta. This paper took away some of the king's power. At first, the rights of the Magna Carta were only for rich and powerful people. But over time, all British people adopted these rights as their own. The British people who left Great Britain for America brought with them the idea that they had rights to life, liberty, and property. They believed that no king could take these rights away from them. They believed that government should work for the good of its people.

Britain's Magna Carta established many principles upon which the Constitution was based.

Most Americans also believed that the purpose of government was to protect people's rights. How could government do that? The delegates once again looked to the British government as a model. They believed that the British system worked because no one part of the government had all the power. The king didn't rule alone. He or his officers could accuse people of crimes, for example, but those accused had the right to a trial. The laws used by the court came from a lawmaking body called Parliament.

The delegates had learned from their experience, however, that a parliament could also become too powerful. They wanted to be sure that the people could always control every part of government.

## Edmund Randolph Proposes a Plan

The first complete plan came from Edmund Randolph of Virginia. Randolph's Virginia Plan proposed that the government have three branches, or parts. There would be an *executive* branch, with a president and some other officers, that would run the government.

At the convention, Edmund Randolph proposed the Virginia Plan. This approach suggested that our government have three branches: the executive, the legislative, and the judicial.

A *legislative* branch, or Congress, would make the laws. Congress would have two parts. One part would be a House of Representatives, with members elected by the people of the states. The second part would be a Senate, with members elected by the House. Last, a *judicial* branch would have a court system, with a Supreme Court at the top. The courts would punish people who did not obey the laws.

When Edmund Randolph finished explaining his plan, the delegates realized that this system would do away with the Articles of Confederation. Some were upset by this idea. They believed that Randolph's government would have too much power.

Others didn't like the way the Virginia Plan worked. Randolph's original idea for a House of Representatives proposed that there would be one representative for a certain number of people. This idea worked just fine for a state like Virginia, which had more people than any other state. But delegates from little states such as Delaware and New Jersey were not happy. They said that under the Virginia Plan, the big states would always have their way.

The idea of a president was a big problem for some delegates. They feared that this person could become just like a king. How would such a leader be chosen? How long should such a person serve? What if the person who was chosen turned out to be a bad leader? Shouldn't there be a way to remove this kind of leader from office?

The debate over Randolph's unique plan went on until the middle of June. At that point, a delegate named William Paterson of New Jersey suggested that the convention simply improve the existing Articles of Confederation. Congress would be able to tax, to make rules about trade, and would be able to appoint a group of men to take the place of a president. Each state would have one vote on national matters, but most lawmaking would be done by the states.

William Paterson argued against Edmund Randolph's Virginia Plan, but was eventually overruled.

The delegates rejected this plan and voted for the basic idea of the Virginia Plan. Now came the hard work of deciding just how this kind of plan could be fair to all states. But all the delegates now understood what they were doing. They were writing a completely new constitution for the United States. A constitution is the basic laws and ideas that define a nation's government.

## A Fight Between Big States and Small States

Delegates from the big states didn't want to give up their power. They insisted that states be represented according to their populations. But delegates from the small states said that wasn't fair. They said each state should have an equal voice. One way to achieve this, the small states said, was to give each state the same number of votes in the Senate.

For nearly a month, the delegates could not agree. Outside, the temperatures soared. Inside, sweat poured down the delegates' faces. Tempers flared often. Once, the delegates from several small states became so angry that they threatened to leave the convention and form their own countries.

But in the middle of July, the delegates found a way to satisfy both big states and small states. This agreement came to be called the Great Compromise. A *compromise* is an agreement in which each side gives up something. The Great Compromise set up the Senate as a lawmaking body in which each state

would have two votes regardless of population. In the House of Representatives, each of the members would represent 40,000 people. (Later, this rule was changed to "no more than 30,000 people.")

Once this agreement was reached, the delegates went on to set up the powers of the three branches of government. They also set up a system of *checks and balances,* which made sure that no one branch could ever have complete power over the other two. Here is the way that system works, even today:

• Congress, made up of elected representatives, has the power to make the country's laws and raise taxes. Any suggested law, called a *bill,* has to pass

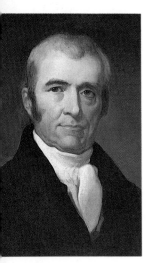

John Marshall was an early chief justice who said the Supreme Court could officially declare a law unconstitutional.

*Opposite:*
A portrait collection of the signers of the Constitution.

both the House and Senate. Then the law is sent to the president for approval. If the president signs the bill, it becomes law. The president can also *veto*, or refuse to sign, the bill. Then the only way the bill can become law is if two thirds of the members of both the House and the Senate vote in favor of it.

• The president's duty is to enforce and uphold the law. The president is also in charge of the armed forces. The president, who is elected for a four-year term, can be removed from office by a process called *impeachment.*

• The Supreme Court, the highest court in the United States, has the power to decide whether a law should be allowed under the Constitution. We say that a law is *constitutional* if it does not violate any of the rules of the constitution. If Congress passes a law, a citizen who believes that the law is unfair may go to court. If the court says that the law is unconstitutional, the law is wiped out and people no longer have to obey it. The power of the Supreme Court to declare a law unconstitutional was not plainly stated in the Constitution. An early chief justice, John Marshall, said the Constitution allows the Court to declare a law unconstitutional. That opinion has been accepted as part of our legal system ever since.

The delegates added a few other parts to the Constitution. For example, they added rules about how old a person had to be to run for the House, the Senate, and the presidency. They decided that anyone who wanted to be president had to have been born in

# 1787 Signers of the Constitution 1937

**GEORGE READ**
Delaware 1733-1798 Lawyer

**GUNNING BEDFORD, Jr.**
Delaware 1747-1812 Lawyer

**JOHN DICKINSON**
Delaware 1732-1808 Lawyer

**GEORGE WASHINGTON**
Virginia 1732-1799 Planter Soldier Statesman

**RICHARD BASSETT**
Delaware 1745-1815 Lawyer

**JAMES McHENRY**
Maryland 1753-1816 Physician

**DANIEL OF ST. THOMAS JENIFER**
Maryland 1723-1790 Planter

**DANIEL CARROLL**
Maryland 1730-1796 Planter

**JOHN BLAIR**
Virginia 1732-1800 Lawyer

**JAMES MADISON**
Virginia 1751-1836 Lawyer

**WILLIAM BLOUNT**
North Carolina 1749-1800 Land Owner

**RICHARD DOBBS SPAIGHT**
North Carolina 1758-1802 Planter

**HUGH WILLIAMSON**
North Carolina 1735-1819 Merchant

**JOHN RUTLEDGE**
South Carolina 1739-1800 Lawyer

**CHARLES COTESWORTH PINCKNEY**
South Carolina 1746-1825 Lawyer

**CHARLES PINCKNEY**
South Carolina 1757-1824 Lawyer

**PIERCE BUTLER**
South Carolina 1744-1822 Planter

**WILLIAM FEW**
Georgia 1748-1828 Lawyer

**ABRAHAM BALDWIN**
Georgia 1754-1807 Clergyman

**JOHN LANGDON**
New Hampshire 1741-1819 Merchant

**NICHOLAS GILMAN**
New Hampshire 1755-1814 Statesman

**NATHANIEL GORHAM**
Massachusetts 1738-1796 Merchant

**RUFUS KING**
Massachusetts 1755-1827 Lawyer

**WILLIAM SAMUEL JOHNSON**
Connecticut 1727-1819 Lawyer

**ROGER SHERMAN**
Connecticut 1721-1793 Shoemaker

**ALEXANDER HAMILTON**
New York 1757-1804 Lawyer

**WILLIAM LIVINGSTON**
New Jersey 1723-1790 Lawyer

**DAVID BREARLEY**
New Jersey 1745-1790 Lawyer

**WILLIAM PATERSON**
New Jersey 1745-1806 Lawyer

**JONATHAN DAYTON**
New Jersey 1760-1824 Land Owner

**BENJAMIN FRANKLIN**
Pennsylvania 1706-1790 Printer

No Known Portrait
**JACOB BROOM**
Delaware 1752-1810 Surveyor

**THOMAS MIFFLIN**
Pennsylvania 1744-1800 Merchant

**ROBERT MORRIS**
Pennsylvania 1734-1806 Merchant

**GEORGE CLYMER**
Pennsylvania 1739-1813 Merchant

**JARED INGERSOLL**
Pennsylvania 1749-1822 Lawyer

**JAMES WILSON**
Pennsylvania 1742-1798 Lawyer

**GOUVERNEUR MORRIS**
Pennsylvania 1752-1816 Lawyer

No Known Portrait
**THOMAS FITZSIMONS**
Pennsylvania 1741-1811 Merchant

the United States, but that other elected officials could be foreign born. The delegates also made rules for how a new state could be admitted to the Union.

Finally, it was time to write the Constitution down. After the delegates looked at the finished document, some were not satisfied. They wanted the Constitution to clearly state the rights of the people, such as the rights to freedom of speech and freedom of religion, in a special part of the Constitution called a Bill of Rights.

But most of the delegates didn't think it was necessary to include a Bill of Rights. When it came time to sign the Constitution, on September 17, 1787, thirty-nine delegates walked to the front of the hall and wrote their names on it.

Many of the delegates, as they signed their names, knew that this was one of the most important moments in history. This group of people, who later came to be called our Founding Fathers, had come to an agreement about how the government of their new nation should work. George Washington declared that the creation of the Constitution was "nothing short of a miracle."

The delegates had kept their work secret for four months. Now it was time to tell the people of the United States just what had happened behind those locked doors in a room in Philadelphia. It was time for the people to decide whether the Constitution would become the law of this new land called the United States of America.

slaves worked on large farms called plantations. These black slaves would not have the right to vote under the new Constitution, because they were not considered citizens of the United States. Delegates from the South wanted to count these slaves as part of their population, so that their states could have more representatives in Congress. But the same delegates didn't want the slaves to be counted for tax purposes.

Today we think of the Constitution as giving all Americans equal rights under the law. But when the Constitution was written, some people counted more than others.

In the new U.S. House of Representatives, the delegates agreed, each member would represent a certain number of people. States that had more people would have more representatives and would pay a larger share of national taxes.

Everyone agreed to this basic idea, but the Southern states had a problem. In the South, many

The delegates argued over this matter for a long time. Then they decided that a state's population would be the total of all "free Persons" plus "three fifths of all other Persons." In other words, a slave would count as only three fifths of a person. It wasn't until after the bloody Civil War that black people would be counted as full citizens in the United States.

# CHAPTER 3

# WILL THE CONSTITUTION BE PASSED?

Americans in 1787 didn't have TV or radio. But news that the Constitution was finished spread like wildfire. Everyone wanted to know what was in this document that had taken so long to write. Within days, debate about the Constitution was raging all over America.

Some people argued that the strong national government described in the Constitution was a good idea. These people were called Federalists because they wanted a strong federal, or national, government. Most people who lived along the Atlantic coastline were Federalists. These people's lives depended on trade with other nations and states, and they thought a strong national government would be good for business.

But many people didn't care about protecting trade. What they feared most was a powerful national government. These people, called Antifederalists, argued that the Constitution would take too many rights away from state governments and also from individual citizens. Many farmers who had claimed land in the western part of the United States, for example, feared that a strong national government would be able to take their land away.

## The Countdown to Ratification

Soon the states began to vote on the Constitution. Each state was to hold a convention to decide whether to *ratify*, or accept, it. If nine states voted yes, the Constitution would become the law of the land.

Delaware, one of the small states that wanted the protection of a national government, was the first to ratify, on December 7, 1787. Pennsylvania, New Jersey, Georgia, and Connecticut had all voted yes by the last days in January 1788. After a month-long convention debate, Massachusetts finally ratified the Constitution on February 6 by a close vote, 187 to 168. Massachusetts also proposed a list of nine amendments to ensure the rights of individuals and of the states. In April, Maryland voted yes, followed closely by South Carolina in May. Then, on June 21, by a vote of 57 to 47, New Hampshire became the ninth state to ratify the Constitution; it too added a list of suggested amendments.

The United States was officially a nation, but so far it was a nation of mostly small states. Without big states like Virginia and New York, the United States would not be very powerful.

Virginia, the state with the largest population, was strongly divided about the Constitution. George Washington, the elected leader of the Constitutional Convention, was from Virginia, but he stayed out of the argument. Patrick Henry, one of the heroes of the American Revolution, was dead set against ratifying the Constitution. He called the document "horridly frightful." Henry feared that the U.S. president could

Patrick Henry was one of the strongest voices against the ratification of the Constitution. He feared that a strong central government would take too much power away from the people.

easily become a king. He also feared that Congress would be able to take too much power away from the people. He warned, "You ought to be extremely cautious . . . for instead of securing your rights, you may lose them forever."

Henry argued powerfully against approving the Constitution. But others, like James Madison, who had helped to write the Constitution, won the day. They assured people that the Constitution would not allow the U.S. president to become too powerful and that the Constitution did not take away too many rights from the states. In fact, Madison said, a strong national government was necessary to protect people's rights. On June 25, the Virginia convention voted 89 to 79 to ratify the Constitution.

## A CELEBRATION IN PHILADELPHIA

The Fourth of July in 1788 was a really special day. Virginia had just become the tenth state to ratify the U.S. Constitution. Just twelve years after the signing of the Declaration of Independence, Americans were celebrating the birth of the United States of America.

In Philadelphia, where the Constitution had been written, people lined the streets to cheer the new nation. Trumpets led a grand parade that lasted all day. A float pulled by six white horses carried a huge copy of the Constitution. Another float held an enormous eagle, the national bird of the new nation. Hundreds of proud new U.S. citizens marched in the parade too. The time for arguing about the Constitution was over. Now it was time to enjoy being Americans!

But like Massachusetts and New Hampshire, Virginia tacked on a list of rights that it wanted added to the Constitution. New York, which also voted yes, by a 30 to 27 vote on July 26, added its own list of rights. By this time, most Americans understood that the Constitution would not be completely finished until a Bill of Rights was added.

Two states did not ratify the new Constitution. North Carolina voted no. Rhode Island, a small state that didn't want to be swallowed up by a big nation, refused to have a convention at all. Eventually, the people of both states would change their minds and join. But no one was about to wait for them. It was time to get on with the business of the nation.

Once citizens learned that the Constitution was ratified, they had great celebrations across the nation.

# Congress OF THE United States

begun and held at the City of New-York, on

Wednesday the fourth of March, one thousand and seven hundred and eighty nine

THE Conventions of a number of the States, having at the time of their adopting the Constitution, expressed a desire... powers, that further declaratory and restrictive clauses should be a... ...confidence in the Government, will best ensure

RESOLVED... ...ted States of America, in Congress a...

...at the following Articles be proposed to the Legislat... ...all, or any of which Articles...

...ures, to be valid to all intents and purposes...

States, pursuant to the fifth Artic...

After the first enumeration requi...

which, the proportion shall b...

until the number of Rep...

nor more than one Repres...

No law, varying the com...

Congress shall make no l...

assemble, and to petition...

A well regulated Militi...

No Soldier shall, in time...

The right of the people...

probable cause, supported...

No person shall be held to an...

Militia, when in actual service...

criminal case to be a witness aga...

In all criminal prosecutions, the a...

district shall have been previously ascer...

for obtaining witnesses in his favor, and...

In suits at common law, where the value in con...

any Court of the United States, than according to the rul...

Excessive bail shall not be required, nor excessive fines imposed, not... ...punishments inflicted.

The enumeration in the Constitution, of certain rights, shall not be construed to deny or disparage others retained by the people

The powers not delegated to the United States by the Constitution, nor prohibited by it to the States, are reserved to the States respectively, or to the

Frederick Augustus Muhlenberg Speaker of the House of Representatives

John Adams V... President...the United States...

# CHAPTER

## 4

# IMPORTANT RIGHTS ARE ADDED TO THE CONSTITUTION

In 1789, the first national elections were held in the United States. To no one's surprise, George Washington was elected president. In his first speech to the nation, he asked the newly elected Congress to consider adding the rights of citizens to the U.S. Constitution.

James Madison, who had played such a big part in writing the Constitution, was a congressman from Virginia now. At first, Madison had not favored a Bill of Rights. He thought that because the Constitution did not give the government a way to take away people's rights, people were protected under the law. But he listened to a friend of his, Thomas Jefferson. Jefferson, who had written the Declaration of Independence about thirteen years before, convinced

*Opposite:*
**The first ten amendments to the Constitution are known as the Bill of Rights. James Madison was very influential in the writing of the Bill of Rights.**

Madison that "a bill of rights is what the people are entitled to against every government on earth."

But what rights should citizens have? Madison had many ideas to choose from. Some states had already made lists of rights. And many people had sent suggestions to Congress. By 1789, some experts say, there was a collection of 211 different rights that people said they wanted.

Madison's list was much shorter. He used the list of rights from his own state, Virginia, as a model. He proposed that seventeen new amendments be added to the Constitution. The Senate and the House of Representatives debated these rights. They finally came up with a list of twelve amendments to send to the states for final ratification.

This process took two years, and two of the amendments were defeated. One defeated amendment was about how many members there could be in the U.S. House of Representatives and how the seats would be divided among the states. The other would have kept pay raises for senators and representatives from taking effect until after an election. The ten amendments that remained became what we call the Bill of Rights.

## What Is the Bill of Rights?

In 1791, the Bill of Rights became part of the U.S. Constitution. What are these rights and why are they important for us today?

**The First Amendment** says that the government cannot interfere with people's rights to freedom of speech, freedom of the press, freedom of religion, and freedom of assembly. It also gives people the right to petition their leaders.

**The Second Amendment** says that because a "well regulated Militia" is "necessary to the security of a free State," the government can't interfere with the people's right to "keep and bear Arms." Arms are guns and other weapons.

At the time the Bill of Rights was written, most men still belonged to their local state militia, or army. They kept their guns at home so they could be ready to defend their country at a moment's notice.

Some people say that because we have no such state militia today, the Second Amendment doesn't give people the right to own guns. But other people say that the Second Amendment guarantees the right to own guns for many purposes, including defense of home and family.

**The Third Amendment** says that, except in time of war, troops cannot be lodged in private homes without the permission of the homeowners. This was included because many people remembered a time when the British had forced citizens to open their homes to soldiers.

**The Fourth Amendment** says that people's homes and possessions can't be searched or taken without an official paper called a *warrant*. A warrant is a document, signed by a judge, that allows police to search for evidence of a crime.  The amendment also says that a warrant cannot be issued without *"probable cause."*  This means that the police must convince a judge that the search of a specific place is likely to produce evidence of a crime.

**The Fifth Amendment** protects people who are accused of crimes.  It says that for a serious crime, such as murder, a person must be charged with the crime by a group called a grand jury.  Twelve to twenty-three people make up a grand jury.  They must examine evidence that the government has against a person and then determine whether there is a strong enough case to charge that person with a crime.

The Fifth Amendment also says that a person can't be tried twice for the same crime and doesn't have to testify against himself or herself.  In a trial, when someone who is on trial refuses to answer questions on the witness stand, we say that witness "takes the fifth."

Another important part of the Fifth Amendment says that no person can be "deprived of life, liberty, or property, without due process of law."  This part of the amendment guarantees all citizens the right to a fair trial before they can be executed, put in prison, or have property taken away from them.  It also means that any laws made in the United States must result in fair treatment of all citizens.

Last, the Fifth Amendment says that the government can't take anyone's property for public use without paying a fair price for it.

The **Sixth Amendment** gives people who are accused of crimes the right to a speedy and public trial by a jury of people from the area where the crime was committed. Without the right to a speedy trial, people could be arrested for crimes and stay in jail for years without ever having the chance to defend themselves in court. The amendment also says that those accused of crimes have the right to know their accusers, to be confronted by the people who have accused them, and to have a lawyer defend them.

The **Seventh Amendment** gives people involved in lawsuits over money or property the right to trial by a jury. It also says that once a decision is made by that jury, the decision can't be changed unless it can be shown that the trial was flawed in some way.

The **Eighth Amendment** protects people who are put in jail. The first part of the amendment says that a judge cannot require "excessive bail" for someone accused of a crime. Bail is money that a person must

During the 1970s and early 1980s, a national movement was organized to support a new amendment to the Constitution. The amendment that was proposed—the Equal Rights Amendment, known as the ERA— would have banned discrimination on the basis of sex. The ERA amendment, however, was eventually defeated.

pay to be freed from jail during the time before a trial begins. The money is returned after a person shows up for trial.

The Eighth Amendment also says that no one can be given "cruel and unusual punishment" for a crime. If a person were convicted of stealing a loaf of bread, for example, it would be cruel and unusual punishment to sentence that person to ten years in jail. The rule against cruel and unusual punishment also prevents such things as the torture of prisoners.

Some people have argued that the rule against cruel and unusual punishment should wipe out the use of the death penalty. A number of years ago, the Supreme Court outlawed the death penalty. But a short time later, the Court reversed its ruling and said the death penalty was constitutional. Many states now allow the death penalty for certain crimes.

**The Ninth Amendment** says that the fact that some rights are not specifically mentioned does not mean that the people do not have them.

**The Tenth Amendment** says that any powers not given to the government by the Constitution belong to the states and the people. This amendment was very important to people at the time the Bill of Rights was ratified. Many people still feared a large, powerful national government, and this amendment put limits on the government.

The Bill of Rights gave citizens of the United States many freedoms and protections that few people in other parts of the world had.

# THE FIVE FREEDOMS OF THE FIRST AMENDMENT

The First Amendment, with its five rights—of religion, speech, the press, assembly, and petition—is one of the most important in the Constitution. Most people in the world do not have the right to say what they want to say, whenever they want to say it. But Americans have that right, as long as their words don't harm others.

The founders valued free speech because it was the free and open debate over problems with England that led our nation to win its independence. Freedom of the press in 1787 was mostly for newspapers and pamphlets. Today, the press includes newspapers, magazines, TV, and radio.

Unlike many people in the world, U.S. citizens have the right to worship or not worship as they choose. The first amendment also says that the government can't have an official church.

**The Constitution protects freedom of religion.**

The right to assemble peacefully means that people may gather in groups for any purpose. U.S. citizens have the right to protest against anything they want to. But courts have ruled that people cannot disrupt traffic or block building entrances. Why not? Because other people's rights would be violated.

What does it mean to petition leaders? You might have seen a table outside a grocery store where people ask shoppers to sign a paper. This paper is called a petition. People often collect a list of signatures on a petition so they can show leaders that a lot of people feel the same way about a certain issue. But a petition doesn't have to be a long list of names. You can write a letter to your senator about an issue. In this way, you are sending a petition to a leader.

# THE CONSTITUTION: A LIVING DOCUMENT

The Bill of Rights didn't make the Constitution perfect. A black slave was still counted as three fifths of a person when the Constitution was written. Native Americans didn't count at all. Women couldn't vote and couldn't even think about running for office. In many states, voting was a right given only to men who had money and property.

The people who wrote the Constitution and Bill of Rights lived in a world that was far different from the world we live in today. They saw the Constitution as being like the foundation of a building. But they knew that the structure built on that foundation would need many changes and repairs.

*Opposite:*
**A giant parade was held in Washington, D.C., in 1987 to celebrate the two-hundredth birthday of the Constitution.**

*41*

The Constitution provides a way to make those repairs in the form of amendments. Amendments can be proposed in two ways. Congress, by a two-thirds vote of both houses, can propose an amendment. Or a national Constitutional Convention can be held, similar to the one held in Philadelphia. So far, all of the amendments added to the Constitution have been proposed by Congress.

To become part of the Constitution, a proposed amendment must be approved by three fourths of the states. Congress may choose to ask state legislatures or state conventions to vote for ratification. So far, all amendments except one have been submitted to state legislatures.

Since the Bill of Rights was ratified in 1791, sixteen more amendments have been added to the Constitution, for a total of twenty-six.

## Some Big Changes in the Constitution

Many of the amendments have reflected big changes in daily American life. After the Civil War, several amendments were written that outlawed slavery and gave all former slaves equal rights under the law, including the right to vote. But the struggle for equal rights for black Americans was far from over. Many Southern states passed laws that made it almost impossible for black people to exercise their right to vote. It took almost another century before these laws were ruled unconstitutional.

After the Civil War, black Americans celebrated the passage of amendments that outlawed slavery.

Another group of Americans, women, also waited a long time to enjoy voting rights. In 1920, the Nineteenth Amendment was ratified, giving women the right to vote in national and state elections. The passage of the amendment was the end of a long struggle called the *suffrage* movement.

Another amendment concerning women was proposed in 1972, but it was defeated after a ten-year battle. This amendment, called the Equal Rights Amendment, or ERA, stated that women should have equal rights under the law.

Only one amendment in U.S. history was first passed, then *repealed*, or rejected. The Eighteenth Amendment was called the *Prohibition* Amendment, because it prohibited, or banned, the making and selling of alcoholic beverages in the United States.

The Supreme Court in 1991. From left: Clarence Thomas, David H. Souter, Antonin Scalia, Sandra Day O'Connor, William Rehnquist, John Paul Stevens, Harry A. Blackmun, Byron H. White, Anthony M. Kennedy.

43

People soon decided that prohibition had been a mistake. In 1933, fourteen years after the Eighteenth Amendment was ratified, the Twenty-first Amendment was ratified. This amendment repealed the Eighteenth Amendment and made the manufacture and sale of alcoholic beverages legal again.

## NATIVE AMERICANS: A SPECIAL CASE

Native Americans lived in North America long before any other settlers arrived. Yet Native Americans have been forgotten people throughout much of U.S. history. Native Americans are mentioned only twice in the Constitution. The first time was in the original Constitution, in the part that sets the rules for counting people to decide how many members a state could send to the House of Representatives. The second was in the Fourteenth Amendment, passed in 1868. Both times, it says "Indians not taxed" are not to be counted as official Americans.

Native Americans in the 1800s.

Native Americans could do little to fight back. They were not officially U.S. citizens, so they were not protected by the Constitution. It wasn't until 1948 that Native Americans gained the right to vote in all states. Twenty years later, Congress passed the Indian Civil Rights Act, which gave Native Americans some, but not all, of the protections of the Bill of Rights.

## The Constitution—Changing, Yet the Same

The Constitution now has twenty-six amendments. Will there be more? Recently, some people have suggested that a children's rights amendment should be added, so that all American children would be guaranteed such rights as food, shelter, protection from abuse, health care, and education.

In your lifetime, it is possible that you will see such an amendment pass. You or your children may even propose an amendment that will further protect people's rights as America changes in the future.

The Constitution of the United States sets out a plan for a government that has worked for more than two hundred years. "We the People" are the only ones who can make sure that our freedom—and our rights—will be preserved.

Today, the Constitution is housed in a special hall in the National Archives building in Washington, D.C.

# Chronology

**1215** King John of England signs the Magna Carta, giving people certain rights to life, liberty, and property.

**1776** American colonies formally declare their independence from Great Britain.

**1777** American leaders sign the Articles of Confederation, sending the colonies into a revolutionary war against the British.

**1786** Shays' Rebellion in Massachusetts makes many Americans realize the need for a federal government.

**1787** American leaders convene in Philadelphia and produce the United States Constitution.

**1789** George Washington is elected the first president of the United States.

**1791** The Bill of Rights becomes part of the U.S. Constitution.

**1920** The Nineteenth Amendment is ratified, giving women the right to vote.

**1933** The ratification of the Twenty-first Amendment repeals the Eighteenth Amendment, which prohibited the sale of alcoholic beverages.

# For Further Reading

Colman, Warren. *The Bill of Rights.* Chicago: Childrens Press, 1989.

Greene, Carol. *The Supreme Court.* Chicago: Childrens Press, 1989.

Rierdan, Ann B. *Reshaping the Supreme Court.* New York: Franklin Watts, 1988.

Smith, Carter, ed. *Governing and Teaching. (A Sourcebook on Colonial America).* Brookfield, CT: The Millbrook Press, 1990.

# Index